Tell Me
What You
CAN
Do

Managing Whatever
Life Throws at You

To Maddy —
Have a wonderful
life!
Mary Beth

Tell Me What You CAN Do

Managing Whatever Life Throws at You

Mary Beth Egeling

Mary Beth Egeling 7/19

Copyright © 2012 Mary Beth Egeling

Library of Congress Control Number: 2012905797

ISBN: 978-1475115963

www.MBEgeling.com

Facebook.com/MBEgeling

Twitter@MBEgeling

In advance praise of Tell Me What You CAN Do

In my real estate firm, things can and do change hour by hour. When this happens, I think of Ms. Egeling's step-by-step approach and say to colleagues, buyers and sellers alike: "Tell me what you can do to get things under control or back on track" or "Tell me what I can do to assist you." By stepping back and saying those few little words, by looking at the big picture for just a second or two before reacting, things do not feel so unmanageable or out of control. I have actually incorporated this method of thinking into my family as well as my business life . . . you can, too!

Tell Me What You CAN Do is an insightful read, showing easy and realistic ways of handling "life's dramas" . . . no matter what is thrown at you, you will learn that you can handle it.

Ellen Carr, Owner/Broker
Smart Real Estate

This book can be an effective resource for creating the results you deserve, no matter what life throws at you. With some simple steps to practice consistently, you can continue to move forward with the important action steps necessary for your success. You'll be grateful to have these tools in your repertoire so you can use them to effectively manage whatever challenges you face. Read this book now, use the strategies, and imagine the possibilities!

Bob Manard
Personal Coach

To my conspicuously absent friend

Jack Kovack

"There is no *try*, only *do*"

I miss you

Foreword

As I began to write this foreword for Mary Beth's book, *Tell Me What You CAN Do*, a serendipitous event occurred. I am a mental health counselor, and one of my clients handed me a calendar written by Louise Hay, who is well known is the healing fields. The calendar's title was "I Can Do It," and contained daily affirmations to remind us of all the things we can do in and with our lives. I chuckled, and the client looked at me, perplexed. I explained to her about Mary Beth's book *Tell Me What You CAN Do* and the uncanny timing of receiving such a calendar.

Tell Me What You CAN Do is an easy-to-understand book that teaches readers to deal with whatever life throws their way by focusing on what is possible, no matter how small the possibilities may be. In my work as a mental health counselor, I often find that patients set unrealistic goals for themselves, only to grow discouraged and quit the task altogether when they fail to reach their own too-high expectations. *Tell Me What You CAN Do* is a book most people will come away from with more awareness on how to focus on the things that

CAN be done in any given situation versus what cannot be done.

My patients grow tired of hearing me say, "It's not that you can't, it's that you won't or don't want to." I am continuously pointing out the phrase "I can't" whenever it is used and attempting to help clients (even myself, my spouse and children) retrain their brains. Research has already proven that our brains can be retrained with repetition and effort. This book is a guide on how we can teach our brains to think differently. By incorporating Mary Beth's ideas from *Tell Me What You CAN Do*, the path to retraining begins!

I especially like the chapter entitled "Do Not Plan Ahead for Emotions that Drain You." As someone who frequently uses what I call "anticipatory anxiety" (this is not a term I coined or developed) this chapter spoke to me. Anticipatory anxiety is exactly what Mary Beth describes in this chapter. It is about anticipating what an outcome will be, and then practicing all kinds of responses as a way to rehearse or plan for what might be coming. Is this a drain on emotion and energy, as Mary Beth states? Yes, it absolutely is, and she explains why from a physiological point of view. Our bodies respond to the thoughts that are put in front of them. When expending energy planning out the worst-case scenario, our body does what it is supposed to do by preparing itself. Is this a waste of energy? I do believe there is usefulness in rehearsing for certain situations, so I do not believe it is an entirely "bad" strategy. The problem lies in using it all the time, in every situation (i.e., as your only strategy or tool to cope). Mary Beth talks about a term she calls the "innerverse" initially in the chapter "Do Not Panic." Becoming aware of this term and the power of the innerverse can certainly help with those of us who struggle with anticipatory anxiety. Once again, we must retrain our brains.

My spouse's first response upon hearing the title of the book was, "My whole life has been the exact opposite." A perfect book for him! I then decided to ask our 9-year-old daughter what the book title meant to her. She replied, "Believe in yourself and see what you can do." Now my curiosity was piqued, so I asked our 7-year-old son what the title meant to him and he replied, "Believe in your dreams." I liked their optimism and automatic thoughts that they could do whatever they tried to do if they simply believed it to be possible.

Many times clients ask me "What can I do?" from a victim's perspective, or say to me, "Tell me what to do." I will keep multiple copies of Mary Beth's book readily on hand for those occasions. Although there have been numerous books written on the subject of positive thinking and learning optimism, *Tell Me What You CAN Do* makes the process simple and straightforward. This is not an intimidating book with page after page of unnecessary rhetoric. Mary Beth gets to the point quickly and her step-by-step approach makes the process easy to put into practice quickly.

This is the perfect book for anyone whose vocabulary is dominated by the phrase "I can't." It is for all those ruled by the fear of trying and failing. I will reference and recommend this book on a regular basis—I believe you will find it both informative and helpful as a practical and positive application to your daily life.

Anne Lenox, LMHC, NCC, CEAP, SAP
Licensed Mental Health Counselor

Before We Get Started

Dear Intrigued and Courageous reader,

I never have and never will take any credit in saying that the basic premise of this book is my original idea. It is not.

During the events leading up to the writing of this book, a simple realization hit me: the conquering-strength-of-the-human-spirit-in-the-snarling-face-of-adversity embodies a unique, innate human characteristic; one we all have hard wired within us, one we all can develop. Sure, some of us are better at this than others, but our abilities in this area can be significantly improved if we work at it.

Much has been written on what I will loosely yet collectively refer to as "the power of positive thinking". But for many of us (including me at certain times in my life) this phrase means absolutely nothing.

How do we get to the point where positive thinking becomes second-nature? If positivism is not an initial or natural reaction to adverse circumstances, how do we learn to take a proactive approach to the trials of living this life?

And yes, I am mainly addressing the tribulations of existence because, let's face it, most of us don't have too much difficulty dealing with the wonderful occurrences that life hands us.

What you will find in these pages is my approach to this innate yet oft untapped ability, an instructional manual, if you will. I will simply share how *I* applied the governing concept of optimism to *my* life; how I integrated the process to work, for *me*. I like a plan. I like predictability. I like to work from a template. Simply stated, this is what I offer you.

What follows is my interpretation of "the power of positive thinking." These are the steps I outlined and compiled, so that it might work more dependably—for my life. This is how the method has worked for me. I believe it will work for you, too.

Best of luck to you; I know you CAN do it!

Mary Beth

Contents

Try

A long while ago, I was put in an amusing yet clarifying and truly life-changing situation which served as the pertinent precursor to *Tell Me What You CAN Do*—it subsequently formed the scaffolding of this, the following effective approach to managing whatever life threw at me.

I was working in a dental office at the time. The owner of the practice, the dentist, was not happy with what he perceived to be a lack of staff concern for his financially lean run of months. He hired a motivational speaker to come in and give a half-day seminar on performance and incentive. The touted results were to improve team efficiency and increase production. His hope was that through the staff's exposure to this presentation, we would somehow become motivated to make more money for him.

During the presentation, the speaker asked for a volunteer from the employees. Since I was already bored out of my skull and looking for a diversion, I raised my hand. I navigated my way through the chairs and chuckles of my coworkers to get to the front of the room, where he was standing next to a small table adjacent to a makeshift podium.

After he asked my name, he proceeded to pull a five dollar bill out of his wallet. He placed the note on the table and looked at me. I looked at him. He looked around the room and smiled—it was the kind of smile that told me *he knew* we were entering into a demonstration where *he* would look better than I did when we were done with whatever it was "we" were going to do. I smiled back, deciding to be a good sport and play along. He put his hand on my shoulder and told me that he wanted me to try and pick up the five dollar bill and that when I did, I could have it.

Of course, I reached for the money. As I was about to put my fingertips on the corner of the bill, he pushed my hand away in a very dramatic manner. My look of confusion was accompanied by amused murmurs from the people with whom I worked.

"No, no," he said with a smirk. "I didn't tell you to *pick up* the money, I told you to *try* and pick it up." The murmurs of my coworkers turned to chuckles; I was amused as well. Now," he said, "I will give you another chance." He looked at me, this time very pseudo-sternly, and said, "Mary Beth, I want you to *try* and pick up that five dollar bill."

I sighed and smiled and shrugged, and again reached for the money. This time when I was just about to touch the bill, he batted my hand away in a spectacular manner. Everyone laughed. I crossed my arms over my chest, indicating that I would not do *that* a third time.

"No, no!" he bellowed with his arms waving in the air. "I didn't ask you to pick up the money!" He then concluded theatrically, "I asked you to **try** to pick it up!"

I'm ready to sit down now, I thought. He asked the audience to give me a "nice round of applause" while he motioned for me to take to my seat. He then struck a very serious posture and poised himself intently on the edge of the platform. He paused. We waited.

I must admit, I do not remember everything he said; it was too long ago. I now paraphrase and offer bits and pieces of his soliloquy—you will get the basic idea.

He proceeded to tell the now-intrigued group that the word "try" means inaction. It means non-function. It means "attempt". When "try" is used, it is most often followed by collapse. It is like embracing failure, welcoming defeat.

He offered the example of how, when we don't really mean to do something, we are apt to say we will "try" to do it. "I will *try* to get home on time." "I have a busy week, but I will *try* to make it to your Tupperware party." Or "I will *try* to get the leaves raked before the game starts." He glanced around the room, looking at a few of us. "I will *try* to get set up for the next patient before I go to lunch." (Hint, hint . . . clearly an example planted by the dentist.)

He briefly discussed the notion of "try" vs. "do." He suggested to us that while at work we take the word "try" out of our vocabulary and make the decision to actually "do" all those things that our varying job descriptions dictated—in actually executing them, we would find ourselves being more efficient, and subsequently more productive.

I worked hard not to roll my eyes. I glanced subtly over at the dentist. He was beaming—clearly liking the outlined plan to get his employees to work smarter and make more money for him. Yeesh. The revealed conspiracy was interrupted by the announcement that it was time for a short break. Good timing.

As the others bum-rushed the bagels and cream cheese, I sat quietly for a few moments. Clearly, the speaker was there to serve in the best interest of the person who hired him. I knew he was not there to work through the legitimate employee concerns that accompanied the perceived lack of staff productivity; it seemed an ambush, a one-sided, the-problem-is-with-all-of-you exposition. Even so, the concept that he briefly introduced (albeit for someone else's monetary gain) profoundly resonated within me.

I must admit I didn't hear much of what the speaker said for the rest of that morning. I may have been mandated to sit there, but I did not have to listen any longer. I sensed that I could, in fact, take away something very valuable from this cheesy seminar; something very precious, indeed. Determined to define what I sensed to be there, I spent the remainder of my time as captive inside my head. And deep within my heart.

That small section of the speaker's presentation forced me into a critical review of my history. I realized that relative to how I lived my life, he was in fact correct about my use of "try." The many times I had used the word "try," I either did not feel I could do something, or I had absolutely no intention of doing what I said I was going to "try" to do.

Long before my days as dental-hygienist-turned-massage-therapist and prior to publishing a single word, I was a writer at heart: I have always loved words; I am still enamored with the connotations and the subtle meanings and inferences they carry when they are pronounced or printed; the conjecture and presumption they provide. I found myself saying the word "try" over and over again in my head. It had a weak sound. Ineffective, wasted and futile. Lame.

I began to think about replacing the feeble word "try" with something more positive and authoritative. The word "will" came to mind. Now *that* is a word!

When preceded by "I," this becomes an unstoppable phrase—"I will"—a definitive statement, one which holds much power and weight. When we say "I'll try," we are building in an automatic excuse. When we say "I will," our statement becomes more binding, much more imperative. It is a commitment. It tells others as well as yourself that something is going to get done.

That very afternoon I forced a paradigm shift in my vocabulary. I vowed never to use the word "try" again. I was either going to *do* it or I was *not* going to do it. There would be no gray area, no in-between. I would make a choice between "do" or "not-to-do."

Something amazing happened when I put this modification into place. I actually started to get more things done! An invisible determination fueled me and I liked it. This new habit also forced me to be honest about those things that I did not want to do, or realistically could not do, but wanted someone else to believe I would. It mandated me to be honest with myself; obligated me to make choices. And making choices for yourself is a very empowering affair as well. It is amazing what happens in your life when you shed the heavy cloak of indecision. You will move and act more effectively. It will literally set you free.

Since this worked so well for me as an important part of an effective approach for managing whatever life threw at me, I decided to integrate this concept into my parenting, thus passing this self-fulfilling, full-steam-ahead strategy on to my daughters—I see advantages of this application in their lives as well. (Seemingly now, I had found yet *another* way to annoy my children—honestly, I do not do it on purpose; it just seems to happen naturally!)

Think of your own life and the many times you have said you will *try* to do something. If you are anything like I was, you will find that a low percentage of those things you "tried" to do did not get done well, or most often, not at all.

My friend Kovack, to whom this book is dedicated, has a saying: "There is no *try*, only *do*." I would like to add to his succinct words: "There is no *try*, only do and *didn't do*."

It Is What It Is

Life is hard. There is no doubt about it. As humans, we struggle daily and eternally with acceptance of this undeniable fact. It is not going to change, so we might as well get used to it; learn to survive —even thrive—during hardships.

The most basic of psychiatry tenets state that avoiding discomfort, disappointment and discord is one of the main reasons for the occurrence of personality disorder and dysfunction in society. If we could just accept the cold reality that things will not routinely go easy and deal with what is relentlessly put before us, we would undoubtedly do better than when we do not.

Humans are gifted and simultaneously cursed with an amazing characteristic: we possess the ability to hold a perception. I am not talking about the "glass-half-full/glass-half-empty" interpretation, or the "half-dozen of one/six-of-the-other" perception. I am speaking about our tendency as humans to mentally alter a reality to meet our presiding emotional or intellectual state. Remember, the Universe presents only facts. It is our *perception* of said facts that causes us to react (or not react) in a certain manner.

We do not like to be wrong. We do not like to think that we have a poor handle on those components that comprise our day. If we have anticipation or desire of an outcome concerning any situation, our ego has much at stake to make sure that the result matches the expectation or hope that our ego harbors.

Our ego does not like to lose. It does not like to be told it is wrong. It does not like to deviate from the plan it neatly lays down far ahead of events yet to transpire. The ability of our ego to perceive events accurately is extremely narrow, often clouded, most times jaded, and almost always stale. It is the part of us that is least progressive, least apt to embrace a shift when necessary from what it "knows" to be true or wants to be so.

Failure to see accurately any circumstances before us can either result in the wrong reaction or, worse yet, no reaction. For there is only one thing worse than seeing a problem inaccurately, and that is not seeing it to begin with.

True, misjudging a situation will most often result in an ineffective or inappropriate reaction. But at least when you apply a wrong reaction to any situation that clearly needs correction, you see that the solution has not presented itself and the resulting inadequacy forces you to come up with another possible course of action. However, not seeing a problem always results in inaction. Do not start your raft down that notorious river of "de Nile": Denial is your worst enemy!

So what does all this have to do with *Tell Me What You CAN Do*, you ask? Everything! Accurate vision will most often result in a move toward an appropriate response. Inaccurate perception will always result in the ever-inappropriate non-response. It is that simple. When distilled to this point, it is easy to see why one must learn to see happenings *accurately and for what they are*. It is important to have precise vision so that you can manage whatever life throws at you.

Interestingly and most often, when we do not like something that is placed before us, it is usually an indicator that our ego is in conflict with a fact presented by the Universe. Disappointment, disagreement or pain (either emotional or physical) over a circumstance means that whatever-the-case-may-be is not turning out the way we want it to.

It is time to pay attention! This uncomfortable reaction is usually a strong indicator that we need to work get clear vision. It is most often a challenge to disengage our ego and accurately assess the situation at hand. In order to move on to successful application of **Tell Me What You CAN Do**, you must be able to look at any given situation, like it or not, and be able to declare the following:

Okay. It Is What It Is . . . *now* it is time to take action.

Do Not Panic

Now hold on . . . just one more thing before you take action. That's right; there is one thing you do *not* want to do prior to doing the things you *do* want to do.

Having accurately and aptly assessed whatever life has thrown at you, it is critical that you Do Not Panic! For when you panic, you stop thinking. And this is *exactly* what you do not want to happen at this crucial, pivotal point.

Unfortunately, when you identify any upsetting reality, the recognition of it does not necessarily insulate you from the "Oh, No!" feeling that often follows. The natural and most common reaction to any clarified, unsettling event is to fall into the trap of being stuck at the point at which the realization comes through . . . panic can and *most often does* result in a paralyzed state. You must get past this place!

In order to do this, as well as ward off alarm at the initial sting of the painful realization, you must force yourself to take a long, deep, slow breath. Hold it in your chest for a few moments as you slowly close your eyes. Release the retained breath in an even, relaxed manner and open your eyes after you complete the cycle. If the news initially *seems* like it is really stressful, do this again—maybe even a few times.

The value of a deep breath is certainly underestimated and commonly undervalued. It does work, albeit momentarily, to ground your body and center your mind. These first seconds are extremely critical because it is a lot harder to come back from a panic than it is to work forward from a stable physical and emotional state. If you can stave off panic in the first few stabbing moments of any distressing reality, you have already beaten the odds of having panic set in!

It is important to understand that the internal space and span of the body has great impact on how we subsequently react to any given stimulus. In serious conversation have referred to this animated, most-intimate space as the *innerverse*: literally meaning the *inner* uni*verse.* Taking a deep breath allows your innerverse to initiate an optimal biochemical chain of events.

Without going into to a lot of complicated biochemistry, the innerverse is an ever-changing sea of billions of cells, hundreds of chemicals and tens of hormones. The nuances of the many reactions that occur literally within split-seconds of any cognitive realization are truly astounding and can only be defined as a cascade of miracles. Suffice to say for the context of this, the *Do Not Panic* chapter, if you can start your innerverse down the path of a calm biochemical reaction, it will pave the way for much of the same to follow—internally as well as outwardly.

With this in mind, a serious caution applies here: similarly, if you allow your innerverse to biochemically jolt toward panic, reactions dictating much of *this* emotion will continue to follow. Yet another good reason to take a deep breath.

All right—you have managed to take a deep, cleansing breath after a grim reality hits you—good job! You have succeeded in securing your innerverse in a positive biochemical send-off towards the next step. It is now time to challenge yourself; to move toward figuring out what you *can do* about whatever life throws at you.

Things are Not Always as They Seem

There is one thing I would like you to keep in the back of your mind before you move to the next step as you learn to manage whatever life throws at you. I want to share a quick story with you to help you keep panic at bay to help put things in perspective relative to the time continuum to which we are all subject. Use the awareness gained from the following tale and apply it as an adjunct at the *Do Not Panic* stage to assist in tempering your reaction to any given situation.

I have heard this tale told many times, with many variations, and in context to many circumstances. As simply and succinctly as possible, here it is:

The Boy and the Zen Master

There once was a boy. On his birthday, he got a horse. Everyone in the village said, "How wonderful!"

The Zen Master said, "We'll see."

Soon after, the boy fell off the horse and broke his leg.

Everyone in the village said, "How terrible!"

The Zen Master said, "We'll see."

Soon after, a war broke out and all the young men were conscripted to fight, but the boy didn't have to go because his leg was broken. Everyone in the village said, "How wonderful!"

The Zen Master said, "We'll see."

Long-range awareness such as this is what you must keep in mind when choosing your reaction to any circumstance. Remember, the Universe presents only facts: it is our perception of them that oftentimes leads us awry. Often, something that initially seems terrible turns out to be a blessing. And at times, a seemingly benevolent event produces an unfortunate outcome. So, as far as how you will eventually be affected by whatever life has thrown at you . . . We'll see.

Do Not Plan Ahead for Emotions that Drain You

—Anger—

"I will be very upset if Joanne doesn't do what I asked her to."

"I will be so mad if I can't find my car keys in the next few minutes."

"I'm going to be very pissed off if I don't get that package today."

"I'm going to get really angry if you say that again."

"I will be furious if this deal falls through!"

—Sorrow—

"I will be so sad if he ever leaves me."

"I will be very disappointed if I don't get this job."

"I will be miserable if it rains on my wedding day."

"I will be depressed if I can't lose ten pounds by my vacation."

"I will be inconsolable if I don't pass my State Board exam!"

Oh my. I truly cannot imagine a more futile, more fruitless endeavor than planning ahead for emotions that drain you. Don't worry—if whatever you think is going to happen does, eventually you'll experience the emotion anyway.

Why rush to get there? If "it" doesn't ever happen, then you haven't wasted energy and effort prior to knowing for sure if it will be necessary to do so.

We all have just so much energy. Don't misuse it, don't squander it—conserve it and preserve it. For when it really counts, you will need to call upon your daily pre-allotment of valuable, expendable power.

We have all said things such as those statements in the beginning of the chapter—it almost seems to be inherent in human nature to immediately expect that things will go awry, because oftentimes they do! This tendency is actually a weak, contrived protection of and for our infantile, fragile egos. But gratefully, there is a way around this unfortunate predisposition.

A better approach is to know and accept that anger and/or sorrow may be a forgone conclusion as a result of virtually any happening, and just put this fact in the back of your mind in the "It Is What It Is" category. Deal with it when and *if* it comes. And not a moment before.

Do not take on the heavy burden of pre-experienced anger and sorrow. For when you choose to use negative vocabulary, either spoken or in thoughts, two things happen. Primarily and most importantly, when you talk to yourself in advance about these energy-draining emotions, your body feels, albeit a slight amount of it, the *actual emotion* of what you are speaking—when the mouth reveals, the body feels.

This is the innerverse we are talking about again. The physiology of your body is connected to your mental state and responds to the words you choose to utter or think. Yes, it is true. This is hard to believe, but put some trust in it. There is a distinct physiologic advantage to keeping your body chemistry out of this emotion-draining realm—until such time you find that you truly do need to be there.

Secondly, the known precept of *The Law of Attraction in the Universe* comes into play here as well. The language and word choice that precede any event have great power and influence on what results afterwards. If you call upon anger, you increase the chances of anger to follow. If you hearken sorrow, like usually follows same. Misery calls more out misery . . . anguish facilitates a similar state. What you call upon will indeed come.

I'm talking quantum physics here; specifically referencing a phenomenon of anatomic particle dynamics. Are you ready for this? Without going into too many truly-hard-to-wrap-your-mind-around details, it has been discovered and subsequently proven that the way certain particles of matter are viewed *actually determine what they turn out to be*!

Yes, it is true—do not doubt it for a minute. As incredulous and preposterous as it may sound, the way something is regarded has a profound effect on how it behaves and how it actually comes out! Does that blow your mind or what?

Okay. Calm down. It actually gets more amazing than this! What is true for the nanocosm of particle physics is true for the microcosm of the innerverse. What holds fast for the human body's innerverse applies to the macrocosm of our world. Anything and everything is connected and strictly acts on this premise. All is beholden to the same rule!

So, how do we alter our approach given the influence of vocabulary and the desire to avoid pre-planning of emotions that drain us? Simple: Word choice and implication. We replace negative words with ones that are positive and imply success.

Let's take two of the examples from each energy-draining emotion listed at the beginning of the chapter. In the following examples, I will change the statement to take into account the two critical tenets: The innerverse's reaction to negativity and The Law of Attraction in the Universe.

—Anger—

"I will be very upset if Joanne doesn't do what I asked her to."

becomes

"I will be very pleased if Joanne does what I asked her to."

"I will be mad if I can't find my car keys in the next few minutes."

becomes

"I will be so happy if I can find my car keys in the next few minutes."

—Sorrow—

"I will be so sad if he ever leaves me."

becomes

"I will be content if we stay together forever."

"I will be very disappointed if I don't get this job."

becomes

"I will be ecstatic if I get this job."

In each of the new examples, not only are you removing yourself from experiencing a stressful bio-chemical shift in your physiology, but you are also increasing the chances of having the situation turn out the way you want.

Now just for practice, go back and apply this word-crafting technique to the remaining examples under each energy-draining emotion, and then return to the next paragraph.

∞ ∞ ∞

How did you do? It really is pretty easy. The true challenge is applying this concept in the heat of the moment, when you are experiencing the situation real-time and have a significant and vested interest in the outcome. Let us be frank—you really do not care that much if it someone else fails their State Board exam, but you certainly would like to pass *yours*.

Like integrating any new habit, this approach takes some practice. If you find yourself uttering any negative "I will" statements (remember as well the power of *these* words), just correct it on the spot and move on. Eventually you will immediately choose the preferred verbal or thought response to the negative stimuli in your life. It will become second nature to use this technique to help you manage whatever life throws at you—applying this concept can not only change your world . . . it can change our world!

Remove Yourself from Victim-hood

For some unknown reason (maybe someone out there can help me understand), there are times we seem to like to be victims. We like to cry woe-is-me and feel sorry for ourselves. We love to receive pity.

Amazingly, during periods of crisis, we do not really *want* help. It annoys us when someone offers what seems to be a viable way out of our professed difficulty. We actually get mad at people who offer a solution! We do not want to know that with a little effort, we can actually solve our own problems—without help from anyone else.

When my daughter Shannon was a baby (and even on up through her toddler years), she had what seemed at the time a peculiar habit. Occasionally, she would find herself upset or enraged or sad or tired. On the realization that she was experiencing any of these emotions, especially the ones that elicited tears and contorted facial expressions, she would rush to a mirror to look at her face while experiencing her agony.

I would observe her doing this very strange thing; watching her red face in the crib mirror and later, more comprehensively, in the dressing-mirror hanging on the back of her bedroom door.

As any attentive mother would do when her child was upset or scared or tired or crabby, I would move to comfort her. I would pick her up and walk her and bounce her and soothe her. I found that after she would begin to calm down, Shannon would work to catch a glimpse of her face in any available reflective surface in the room. If I put her back in her crib, she would waggle over to the mirror so she could see her face. If I put her back on the floor, she would crawl over to her reflection on the back of the door. As soon as she was able to secure a surface in which she could see herself, she would ceremoniously cry or wince or grimace for a few moments while she watched herself. I usually observed these antics with slight amusement, joined by some confusion and befuddlement.

Shannon quickly outgrew this need to keep herself in view while she was angry or sad or suffering. Sadly, many of us never exhaust this infantile tendency; we just learn to hide our antics better. Even when a solution presents itself, the need to continue to bear witness to our own suffering remains.

Perhaps on some level we want other people to solve our problems for us, but only after some cajoling or convincing from them. Perchance we are for some reason reticent to allow ourselves be the solution to our own issues. If you suffer from this tendency, you must get past this place! Allow me to offer the last stanza from a poem I wrote many years ago, which suggests the solution to just this exact stuck point:

> *The bars—you stare from*
> *The prison—you choose*
> *The key—in pocket*
> *Decision—to use.*

Now . . . get that key out of your pocket and let's learn how to use it.

We are Actually Hard-wired to Succeed

As if the biochemical reaction of your innerverse is not amazing *enough*, let us further bolster the convincing argument for adopting the ***Tell Me What You CAN Do*** approach to whatever life throws at you: Your neurophysiology also comes into play in a very significant way. We are actually hard-wired to succeed!

To understand this concept, we must first briefly (and I mean briefly) explore the concept of **neuroplasticity**. Neuroplasticity loosely and very basically refers to the brain's ability to organize and reorganize itself in response to events or experiences. The areas of our brains that house the distinct centers for emotional response and the potential to implement it are inexplicably linked—they have direct communication with one another by way of neurological pathways made up of specialized cells named **neurons** and the space between them, called **synapses**.

With this intimate relationship between these two neural parts, our brain can literally systematize itself to see the glass as "half empty," or arrange itself to view it as "half full." And as we all know from personal experience, those who see the water *in* the glass and not what is missing *from* it are most likely to come out ahead. Defeatist or opportunist—the choice really is yours.

Our attitude and perception about an event and the language we choose to describe an experience directly influence future outcomes. Any direction in thinking, both positively *or* negatively, grows and strengthens connections between brain cells that influence effort and motivation.

Simply stated, one who thinks positively will have more motivation and gumption than one who thinks negatively. The person who chooses to think positively will have drive and enthusiasm. The negative person will be de-motivated and without energy. You may be nodding your head—your intuition tells you that this is indeed so. You know people like this on both side of the spectrum! Yet again, like attracts same!

Interestingly and thankfully, although childhood is certainly the best time to positively arrange these pathways, this pro-genesis is not relegated to the young, developing brain. There is ample evidence giving credence to the fact that neuroplasticity can be and is in effect in the mature brain as well. At any age, we can actually affect and be conscious facilitators in the reorganization and reinforcement process that is defined by the phenomenon of neuroplasticity.

Importantly and as an aside, we cannot think of two things at once. It is not possible for our brains to entertain two concurrent thoughts. We can alternate very quickly between thoughts, we can choose one or the other to think about with a split-second between them, but cannot think of two separate entities at the same time. It is simply not possible.

Use this neuro-physiologic fact to your advantage: Energy being expended on one channeled thought cannot be spent on another. Choose to spend your thought energy on an optimistic perspective.

Keep this fact in the not-too-far-from-your-conscious space. Do not forget that we are actually hard-wired to succeed!

In the immortal and forever-topical words of Henry Ford: "Whether you think you can or think you can't . . . You're right!"

Putting it all Together

Revisit the discussion of perception, It Is What It Is—the Universe presents only facts. Recall, if you will, Do Not Panic—you can biochemically put yourself in a position to prevent panic from happening in the first place. Remember that things are not always what they seem and do not immediately decide if any given event is "wonderful" or "terrible"—we'll see. Reexamine the reality that the way something is seen determines how it turns out—your perception can actually impact outcome (quantum physics for daily application). Remember not to plan ahead for emotions that drain you and remind yourself that you will not be a victim. Recollect that you are actually hard-wired for success.

Put this together and what do you have? Go ahead . . . you are smart! You already know the answer: You have at your command a solid way to shape your own day. A dependable method to determine your own destiny. A cache of tools to scaffold your approach. A comprehensive trust of invaluable tenets to temper your reactions.

You are now ready—really ready—to proceed to managing whatever life throws at you. We can finally move on. It is time to tell yourself what you can do.

Tell Me What You CAN Do

Everything you have learned prior to this point will wipe the slate clean and give you great advantage over your situation. You have put it all together. You are now in a state of lucid, grounded reality; an ideal point from which to proceed. Congratulations are in order— many do not ever get to this point. You are intrigued. You are courageous. Do not stop now.

Know that being able to get to this point has already ensured the odds are in your favor that you will successfully solve your problems or correct your issues. When you command yourself "Tell Me What You CAN Do," this significant declaration and what naturally follows sheds light on a seemingly dark situation. It opens up possibilities. It literally buys you the precious commodity of time. And as you will soon find out, time is really all you need!

Okay. Now you can actually exclaim to yourself and others around you: Tell Me What You CAN Do!

Asking Others

If you are feeling very adventurous at this juncture, skip to the next chapter and return to this one when you are done (but don't forget to come back). Start reading again at the asterisk in the margin, which indicates the this-is-where-the-adventurous-people-pick-up-the-chapter spot. If you are feeling intrigued but kind of tentative and wish to move along in order, do not feel bad; that's Okay too . . . keep on reading!

Asking someone else to "Tell Me What You CAN Do" is much easier than asking the same question of yourself. Typically there is less emotion involved. Problems that other people have are not usually as imperative and unsettling as the ones we experience ourselves. It may seem out of the natural order to start applying the concept to other people first, and this may very well be the case.

However, some individuals do not want to jump right into managing whatever life throws at them. Perhaps you prefer to ease into something, help someone else; see immediate, concrete results and gain an advantage. Go to school on them, so to speak. Make sure that it works for *them* before you test the theory on yourself.

Asking this question of someone else in their time of need—prior to undertaking this application with your own life situations—can help introduce others to this concept *and* do much to bolster your own faith and subsequent success in the process.

* (Okay, this is where the adventurous people pick up the chapter.)

When you ask someone else to "Tell me what you can do," you are essentially directing the sequence of events that *should* transpire during the process of application of the **Tell Me What You CAN Do** approach to managing whatever life throws at them.

For the sake of example, let us explore the following possibly common and totally probable scenario. Take your roommate, for example, who is getting ready to go to work. After announcing he is leaving for the day, he goes out to find that the car has a flat tire. The ensuing dialogue might go something like this:

> **Your Roommate:** (Slamming the door while re-entering the house.) "Gosh-darn-it, I have a flat tire! I'm going be late for work—now I can't possibly get there on time! I can't change a tire and I'm already behind at work and I can't believe this is happening to me and I really do *not* need this right now and this

is the worst day ever and my life is one big mess and I can't even *take* it any more!" (Chest heaving for emphasis)

You: (In a very soothing voice) "Now, just take a deep cleansing breath and calm down." (You are clearly at a disadvantage here since panic has already set in. But you can still help salvage this situation.) You continue: "I'm sorry that you have a flat tire, but *It Is What It Is,*" (pertinent first chapter application), "so you might as well accept it and work on solving the problem." (Caution: after saying something like this when someone is panicking, be warned and be prepared . . . it might get worse before it gets better, or they might get really angry.) While putting your hand up to halt their protest, you continue: "Instead of focusing on the limitations of this problem by telling me what you *can not* do, why don't you Tell Me What You CAN Do. (Ta-Da!)

Your Roommate: (With an incredulous look on his face) "Have you lost your mind?"

You: (Shaking your head 'no' and repeating yourself calmly) "Instead, just Tell Me What You CAN Do."

Your Roommate: "What the heck is going on?"

You: "No, really. Tell Me What You **CAN** Do."

One of three things will happen here. One, your roommate will say nothing and continue to stare at you blankly. Two, (the least likely possibility of the three) your roommate will actually stop whining, think about his situation and tell you what he can do (perhaps because he's so stunned he does not know how to else to react, and *possibly* to shut you up). Or three, you will have to pick up here at this place because he just told you where to go.

Since number three is the most likely scenario, you are obliged to continue the unsolicited yet very helpful direction and dialogue. This gives you an opportunity to apply the concept with flair and panache, enumerating on the ample list of what can be done.

> **You:** "Well all right, then, *I'll* tell you what you can do." (As you put your fingers up, in front of his face, one by one). "You can ask me to help you. You can call work and tell them you are going to be late because you have a flat. You can call an emergency repair service to fix your tire. You can take your bicycle. You can call a taxi. You can take a half-day off and get some laundry done. You can take my car. You can ask me to drive you. You can call for a bus schedule and . . ."

> **Your Roommate:** (Sighs emphatically) "All right, all right . . . I get it!" (At this point you have offered

so many solutions; he cannot help but give in.) He continues, "I'll let you drive me to work. You are so incredibly annoying—Yeesh!" (Don't expect a thank-you just yet.)

On the way to work you can wax triumphant (in a minimalist sort of way) and point out that *see, it did work out after all*, and that when he gets out of work the flat tire can be definitively dealt with. Crisis averted, problem solved! Bring on the rest of the day!

Ask Others often to tell you what they can do and you will eventually arrive the satisfying point where you will not even have to utter the oft-employed phrase at all. There are few things that irritate my children more than when I repeatedly suggest "Tell Me What You CAN Do." Currently it has gotten to the point where, when the words "I can't" come out of either of their mouths, I only have to form the usual expression in preparation for my irritating axiom, and they hold up their hands and beg me to please *not* utter "that annoying phrase" again!

Asking Yourself

If you decided to jump ahead to this chapter and start by Asking Yourself, I am impressed! Unmistakably, this is the more difficult of the two possible applications of *Tell Me What You CAN Do*. If you are just joining us after reading the last chapter, I am still impressed. Regardless of where you decided to start, know that it takes courage to tackle this section.

And now we come to it. If, even after all the factual and logical information contained herein has been internalized, you still hear yourself *about* to say, or feel yourself *about* to think: "I cannot do whatever-it-is," stop immediately.

Wrap your mind around this: Any inkling plants a thought, and a thought guarantees that expounding on that inkling will follow. Do not focus on what you cannot do; each singular thing you decide you "cannot do" will continue to grow in enormity in your head and invite more negativity.

Remember, like follows same. You are poised to take yourself down a negative path; you are staring down the dark side of the fork in the road. You are initiating talk to yourself in a manner which will ensure that you, the recipient and object of the comments, **will not** be able to do something. And clearly this is not what you want.

Instead, take a deep cleansing breath. Assert to yourself out loud, "Tell Me What You Can Do!" Even though it may seem a bit strange at first, demanding it *aloud* is important until you get the hang of this, as hearing yourself *say* the affirming phrase actually facilitates the shift. In doing so, you attract like forces, and remember, like forces call on much of the same.

And yes, I am asking you to talk to yourself. Self-talk is a powerful thing. It is not silly. It is not a crutch. It is not a sign of insanity. Initiating a self-*conversation* always implies that a response will follow. Do this and I guarantee that one will—one that will be very productive and worth the effort, discipline and energy you expended getting to the point where you call upon yourself to respond to this decisive command in the first place.

Stay calm and be open to what follows. Use your cleansing breaths so that your innerverse remains stable and receptive. Keep and hold the gift of time you have given to yourself so that a solution to your issue has time to materialize. Watch the nothing-short-of-cascade-of-miracles that unfold as a result of your non-judgmental, grounded lucidity.

Make no mistake about it, you are now in a special state of grace . . . and what holds true for this instant can become a template for your lifetime.

There is Always One More Thing You Can Do

Whether Asking Others or Asking Yourself, after a few moments of coaxing conversation about what you can do and yet not coming up with anything you can do, do not get discouraged or, worse yet, say "This stupid approach for managing whatever life throws at me doesn't work!"

You still have given yourself the gift of additional time and you still have options. Remember, the longer the resolution gate is open, the more time and chances there are for solutions to present themselves. Oftentimes an answer does not appear immediately after the problem arrives. Allowing time for the solution to develop is critical for resolution. This is why one must not panic when they ask themselves what they can do and nothing immediately (or even a time after) comes to mind.

Adaptability. Resourcefulness. Ingenuity. This is where these innate yet oft untapped but readily available problem-solving characteristics come into play. And yes, when I say innate, that means that you have them too: not just a few lucky people . . . all humans. True, each of us have these desirable qualities in greater or lesser degrees, but the tendencies are present in everyone. We need to seek them, we need to find them. Recognize that they are there; acknowledge them, develop them, then *use* them.

Interestingly, these problem-solving characteristics manifest themselves best in a non-panic state. I am not saying that any given situation may not be a crisis; it may very well be. But you have managed to secure your innerverse in a state of focused calm, the perfect environment for you to call upon and use these three problem-solving tools.

Someone has to keep their wits about themselves and work through the problem. It might as well be you.

When There Truly is Nothing Left to Do

There is a remote chance that eventually you will run out of things you can do. Finality of *some* remote conditions or situations is, unfortunately, a foregone conclusion. This may seem in direct contradiction to the content of this book, but bear with me.

You must not arrive at this point prematurely, or skip to *this* end. As was already discussed, you might potentially miss a solution to the problem. If you do prematurely end up at this place, initially being defeatist will *ensure* that you will not be able to aptly apply an effective approach for managing whatever life throws at you. Do not run headlong into what from far away looks to be a brick wall . . . let yourself approach it slowly. You may miss a subtle solution along the way which will help you avoid an injurious impact.

Okay. So there is really nothing you can do. Believe it or not, even in the extremely rare event that there is truly nothing you can do, there is *still* one more thing you can do.

Getting Past It

Time to utilize again an application that was introduced at the onset of this book: *It Is What It Is*. Well, here we are: *seemingly* back at the beginning again. You have run through the entire process and there truly is nothing left to do. True, you may ostensibly be in the exact position you were in when you initially come to the conclusion at the *It Is What It Is* juncture. But you have undergone a valuable transformation in the cycle you just completed. You are not right back where you started. You did not turn around in a circle while standing in place. You protected your body, you bolstered your spirit—you rolled forward in the sphere of growth.

When you have truly exhausted all options, even when there is no apparent solution available, you *still* have one choice left. That's right. There is yet one more thing you can do when there is nothing you can do. You can make the choice of what your *attitude* about the situation is going to be.

This may not seem like a choice, but in fact it is. It holds much significance and influence in any inoperable situation that you find yourself in. You must now work to change your attitude.

Changing an attitude is one of the hardest things for humans to do. What this actually means is not only altering your outlook on the matter, but releasing yourself from emotions that drain you—these stagnate when you do not change your mind-set. Changing your viewpoint at this juncture cannot be complete unless you free yourself from emotions that hold you stuck where a bad attitude hangs out and continues to do damage and keep you stuck.

It is easy to harbor resentment, anger, jealousy or sorrow. Don't do it. It casts an anchor on your spirit and puts a great deal of drag on your body. It is like traveling down the river of your life with cumbersome cargo aboard, making it difficult to navigate effectively. Travel light down this life; lighten your load and improve your position so you have the energy needed to cope with and manage whatever life throws at you.

A good, adjusted attitude keeps you fresh, keeps you alert. It keeps that tiny conduit called *hope* open to messages from the Universe. Of course, hope is not synonymous with attitude, but they share a unique direct relationship. Yet another interdependent principle to keep in mind while forever being governed by the Laws of Attraction.

Either negative *or* positive, never underestimate the power of attitude. Your attitude about your situation will either ensure that you will continue to feel agony *over* it, *or* will insulate you *from* it. Let's face it. Attitude is one of the hardest things to change and has the most profound effect on what follows.

The Best Example

"Houston, we have a problem." On April 14, 1970 those immortal words of Commander Jim Lovell echoed across the cold void of space. In my opinion, there is no better example of *Tell Me What You CAN Do* in action than the real-life drama of the Apollo 13 Mission.

I was seven years old when these historical events occurred. My only memory is that of my parents watching the special report on television where Walter Cronkite informed a shocked nation that the Apollo 13 astronauts Jim Lovell, Fred Haise and Jack Swigert were in great danger—that their lives might be lost.

As I got a little older, I came to learn a few additional facts about those long days in which the entire world stood vigil, but truly never realized the literally crisis-driven conditions unfolding behind the scene.

In 1997, the movie *Apollo 13* was released. Artfully directed by Ron Howard, it is, in my estimation, a masterful re-enactment of the Apollo 13 mission and delves into the circumstances of that fateful course of days in 1970. Exhaustive research was conducted, endless interviews recorded, and the result is an *inside* the-inside-story of what really transpired that spring.

Events and conversations were brought to light—ones the public was never privy to until the release of the film. Only after I watched the movie did I truly appreciate the nothing-short-of-amazing chain of events which unfolded before and after the launch.

I will not even make an attempt to retell the entire story. Nothing I could ever offer here would do the actual arduous days any justice. And I am sure that nothing portrayed in the film could come remotely close to approximating the intensity of the drama of the real-time events.

In 1970, Gene Krantz, the director of flight operations at NASA (and in my estimation, the ultimate **Tell Me What You CAN Do** person), is faced with some critical, sobering news. A few days into the mission, during a routine test function, the space capsule experienced a horrific explosion from one of the oxygen tanks. As a result, there were serious mechanical problems and the craft was disabled. Not only was the lunar landing scrubbed, but the ground crew was faced with the daunting task of getting the now-stranded-in-space astronauts back. Alive.

In a single moment, an operation initiated for exploration turned to a challenging rescue mission with the clock racing fast against it. The situation was dismal. It was stone-cold sobering. It seemed beyond hopeless.

Gene Krantz worked tirelessly and consistently with adaptability, resourcefulness and ingenuity (along with positivity and courage) against every single, seemingly insurmountable obstacle that was thrown in front of him. He labored to keep himself in a calm, alert, mindful state. He dealt with one problem after another and would not even entertain a sliver of suggestion of defeat. He rallied the staff of mission control and factored in every option and possibility in the equation. He accepted cold, hard realities swiftly, and his signature approach to problem solving united a group of people to work in such a cohesive manner, they became an unstoppable force.

Director Krantz is quoted as saying such Tell-Me-What-You-CAN-Do things as the following:

"Let's stay cool, people."

"Let's work the problem, people."

"Let's not make things worse by guessing!"

"Let's look at this thing from a standpoint of *status*—
what have we got on the spacecraft that's good?"

"From now on we are improvising a new mission."

"I don't care what anything was designed to do.

I care about what it can do!"

"We never lost an American in space and we are not going to lose one on my watch!"

"Failure is not an option!"

And finally, when one of the NASA directors suggested that if just *one* of the many things that could go wrong during the landing *did*, it "would be the worst disaster that NASA ever experienced," Gene Krantz responded confidently and pointedly:

"With all due respect, sir, I do believe this is going to be our finest hour."

And he was right . . . it was!

This is not to take away from the contribution of the many others who were part of the collective solution. During all this turmoil, Jim Lovell also remains in control of himself during the crisis; he is calm and present to the moment even though *he* is on the ship that is compromised. In spite of the profound disappointment at the fresh realization that he would not ever fulfill his dream of walking on the moon, he had to contend with the sobering fact that he and his crew were stranded in space—still he perpetuates his calm, mindful state.

A member of the original team of three, astronaut Ken Mattingly, was removed from the mission just before launch due to exposure to measles. He was devastated at being taken out of the mission, but it turns out he was part of the critical solution while *remaining on the ground.* Every person involved in the resolution was whipped up and caught in the positive, focused fury of bringing the astronauts home.

If the Apollo 13 Mission events are not familiar to you, do some research or watch the movie. After I saw it, I was stunned. While the credits rolled, I sat motionless in the dark theater—I thought hard. The reenactment demonstrated, like nothing else I could think of, the true power of Telling Others as well as Yourself what you can do.

It reminded me, albeit to a much more profound degree, of how I learned to manage whatever life threw at me. Again, I am not special, I am just doing what I am evolutionarily gifted to do—I simply came up with a dependable template for applying it consistently to my happenings and the results were always desirable. Figuring out what we can do is characteristically unique to humans and it is readily available to all of us to apply to our lives.

I use the Apollo 13 Mission as my touchstone and my reality check. When I have reached the end point any given place in managing whatever life throws at me and there is really nothing I can do, I compare my circumstance to this benchmark situation. Since I cannot possibly think of anything that could be more serious or alarming than the events of those tense days of the Apollo 13 mission, it puts my crisis in perspective. It helps me frame the perceived impact of my fresh lucidity. It forces me to keep my wits and compels me adjust my attitude. Let's face it: *Nothing* that life has thrown at me could ever remotely compare to *that*.

But enough about me—let's talk about you. You are intrigued. You are courageous. There is nothing more we can do together. It is all on you. The time has come for you to Tell Me What *You* CAN Do!

Appendix

Until this process becomes natural for you, I have designed a Quick-reference Flow-card for you to cut out and keep with you. Make copies of it; place them in and around your space . . . put them wherever you can see them, or where they might be available for handy reference: I have one on my refrigerator, one on my desk, one in my wallet and one in my car. Even if you are not undergoing a given moment where you might need to tell yourself what you can do, the constant visual reinforcement is always helpful to your subconscious. It can't hurt and it can only help.

For the sake of decoding this quick-reference flow-card, the arrow symbol represents a *critical turning point* in the process; if you succeed in securing yourself in the state indicated by the arrowed prompt, your chances for success increase dramatically. The checkmarks represent what you do after that point, to ensure continued success until you can get to the next critical phase!

Tell Me What You CAN Do
Quick-reference flow-card

- ➢ **It is What It Is**
- ➢ **Do Not Panic**
- ✓ Things are not always as they seem
- ✓ Remove yourself from victim-hood
- ✓ Remember you are hard-wired to succeed
- ➢ **Tell yourself what you CAN do**
- ✓ There is always one more thing you can do
- ✓ If there is truly nothing more you can do:
- ✓ Compare your situation to the Best Example
- ➢ **Adjust your attitude and get past it**

Acknowledgements

Mary Kathleen Dougherty
My publishing mentor, my colleague

Colleen Dunn
My graphic design expert, my cousin

Lisa Benwitz
My editor, my friend

Heather and Shannon Swenson
My inspiration, my daughters

Michael Rizzo
My partner, my love

NOTES

NOTES

NOTES

NOTES

NOTES

NOTES

NOTES

NOTES

NOTES

NOTES

NOTES

NOTES

NOTES

NOTES

NOTES

NOTES

NOTES

NOTES

From the Author of

Tell Me What You CAN Do

Love-abouts

Can a simple daily activity really enrich your life and deepen your relationships? Yes! It can be easily applied to all interpersonal interactions with great results and success. No exaggeration, "Love-abouts can change your world... maybe even change our world!"

"It's rare that you come across both a simple and powerful message. Love-abouts says so much in such a short space. Over the many years of being exposed to victims of sexual abuse and missing children, I know in my heart that this little message could have saved and healed a lot of these victims. Why, you ask? The reason is open, honest communication and knowing you have the ability to say what is in your heart without fear. What a liberating thought!!! Every family that values each other must read this and begin to start practicing Love-abouts today. Tomorrow is not an option."

~Lou Bivona,
Chairman and Founder National Center
for Missing & Exploited Children for New York
Founder of Bivona Child Care Advocacy Center, Rochester, NY

From the Author of
Tell Me What You CAN Do

MESSAGES FROM MY
HANDS

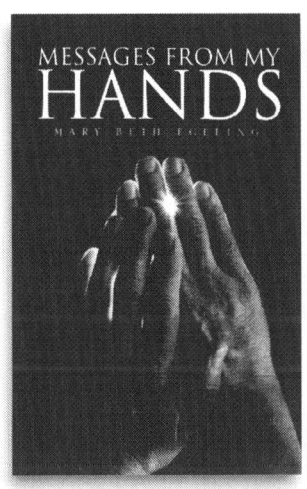

There are forces working within and through our bodies that cannot be seen but unquestionably do exist. The distraction, confusion, and disharmony that define much of our existence overshadows these subtle intrinsic powers. If we learn to pay attention, we can hear them. Ms. Egeling believes the means to challenge personal discontent is encrypted in our bodies and suspended in the dynamics of our simple interactions. *Messages from My Hands* is a compilation of experiences that have collectively coaxed the author from a self-absorbed, self-serving existence. Through the retelling of these compelling, intimate interactions, she explores the thawing of her purpose and liberation from behaviors that were the source of unhappiness and stagnation. Understanding the body and honoring our connection to the universe are two of the fundamentals necessary for change and growth: the wisdom derived from these principles is equally available to anyone who seeks them.

13504201R00066

Made in the USA
Charleston, SC
14 July 2012